LAMENTATIONS
OF A SON

Rex Alphin

First published in 2018 by

Rex Alphin
Zuni, Virginia
United States of America

www.rexalphin.com

Library of Congress Control Number: 2018908220

ISBN: 978-1-64440-387-7

Set in Bembo Std
Printed in the United States of America by Gorham Printing, Inc.

For those who have lost…

Contents

:: I ::

Since My Father Died   1
One More Year   2
Lamentation of a Son   3
The Last Days   4
Finish Line   5
Apprenticed   6
Scents   8
Thankfulness   9
Roots   10
42 Years   12
December   13
Peach Tree   15
Together   17
Next Time   19
Currents   20
Destiny's Cup   21
Rainfall   23
Cessation of Life   24
Late Again   25
Much to My Dismay   26
Tearcatcher   27
Next Tuesday   28
Old Reruns   30
Enigma   31
Survival   32
Chopping Wood   33
Gulag   34

:: II ::

The Backyard   39
Foggy Mornings   40
Morning Rain   41

The Third Day   42
Cows   44

:: III ::

Awakened   49
Dissenter   50
Traveling   51
Trickery   52
Tell Me   53
Tarriance   54
Unhinged   56
Perhaps   57
Beauty   58

:: IV ::

Gravity   63
Life Across the Bridge   64
Vacation List   65
The Tip Jar   66
Dominoes   67
Crestfallen   68
Turning Point   69
Coasting   71
Exiled   72
Sanctification   73
Guests   75
Sibling Rivalry   76
Fissure   77
The Return   78
Ode to Texas   80
Silence   82
Eyes   84
Run With Me   85
Bleeding   86

Foreword

The winter of '17, my father died. It propelled me down a path I had long dreaded but could never have fully comprehended. In the midst of that freefall, I grabbed anything that was still firm—family members, dirt, my Creator, memories and, oddly enough, poetry. This genre seemed to possess the ability to define that which I could not. The effort to write it, the articulation of it all, gave credence. The existence of words on paper that one could see and feel with fingers gave voice to that great vacuum.

Some of the poems to follow are the outworking of that grief. Having discovered this new language, it was natural to pen musings on other subjects. I have tried to cast them in some semblance of order.

Robert Frost once wrote "The utmost of ambition is to lodge a few poems where they will be hard to get rid of…" May you find one or two of these difficult to remove.

:: I ::

Since My Father Died

Since my father died
The farm seems hollow
As it calls out his name
Like a lost child for its mother

The long bond
Formed a generation
Has been broken
As the land yearns and weeps

They shared a love
Few have known
An intimacy
Built on reciprocity

As each gave all he had
For the other
And reveled
In the sacrifice

It grows again,
For him!
A bounty year
It is!

But his eyes
Are not here to see it
Nor his callused fingers
To rub across the kernels
As in all the years past

I weep with the land

One More Year

Having lasted this long
We all thought
The curtain might never fall
And the play go on forever

Not to one
Cut anywhere
Would bleed life

And, having his fair share of brawls
With the enemy
Would he not rise before the count of three
As he'd always done?

Had we known,
Would words be more deliberate
And a vicious clinging
To the laugh
The old stories
The pointed finger?

Would have savored it all the more
Had I known
The sun would set
At such a time

Surely one more year
Would not have been too much
To ask
Would it?

Lamentation of a Son

Yes, feel the pain
That utter emptiness
That comes only from
Such loss

He is gone, I tell you!
Why grieve the night away
And waste those salty tears?
Save them for something that will do some good

Is that not what he taught you
As you both stood betwixt the rows
Making your grand plans
Even as your Creator plotted otherwise?

But even that,
The thwarting of your ambitions
Did its double duty
And brought you closer still

Such it is with shared disappointment
That breathes breath into the bond
In such a way
Successes never could

A many-a season
We made our way
Through all manner of enemies
Who sought to strangle our joy

But their combat was folly
How could they have won?
All such efforts toothless
Against a father/son

The Last Days

'Twas not his natural habitat
This chrome laden jungle
Swept of natural life
Like premeditated murder

No Sunset Views
No golden hues
No cattle on a hill
No skies scanned for thunderheads
No calls of whippoorwill

Would rather have seen
Him plowed under
As he released his grip
On open tractor
And fell into the furrow
While his wife waited
His return
Frying cornbread

I'd heard him say
A thousand times
(he gave it all, no doubt)
But this would be
The last time we would hear
"I'm wore out"

Finish Line

It is now September.
I glance across the rows and fields he once loved
And cry
Again

He resurrected at harvest time
And raised us all to life
That driven, deliberate demeanor
That heaved us all skyward
Like a grand tsunami
As we gasped
And sprinted
And tried to keep up
Straining to glimpse the last row
Collapsing across the finish line

As he rode his chariot
Into our midst
And spoke to us
All known languages
Without speaking

Apprenticed

Immersed in his wake
Unaware the magnitude

Just watching
And being imprinted
Like mimeograph copy

As we sank corner posts
And stretched barbed wire tight
But not too tight

As we set a shed square
And heaved her into existence
Planting trusses
Amongst azure soil

As we plowed the first furrow of spring
Keeping 'er straight
Well,
Fairly straight

As we felled Red Oaks
For winter crackles
And basked
In the effort

As we looked west
With wishful eyes
Always west

As we felt the soil
For all her dispositions
Her warmth
Her moisture

Her pleasure

As we closed out another weary day
Giddy
That destiny
Had dealt us such a hand

Taught me much
And much it was!
Complete 'til final breath
But this one thing
I failed to grasp-
To bear a father's death

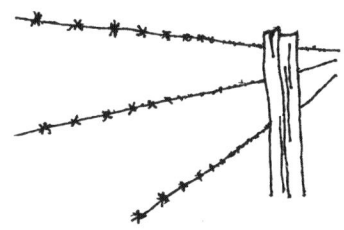

Scents

Striding
Into
Its
Orbit

The olfactories
Resurrect
Echoes
Of another day

That house
That laugh
The calloused hand

The flood
Of recollections
Floats into
The caverns

And identifies
The owner
A way DNA
Never could

Thankfulness

Of thou many endowments
Bequeathed since Adam's fall
None has been more blessed
Than poor recall

Roots

Taught us well, he did
Those eternal July days
When time
Took her time

"Pull it up by the roots"
He directed
"and knock the dirt out"

As we stared down
Another damn row
In dread
The hot sand laughing at our hesitancy

As he plowed ahead
The pace horse
Unaffected (or so it seemed)
By such inferno

Bending at the waist
His brown hands
Grasping another trespasser
His protruding eyes

Scanning for another
As his right hand
Takes his former victim
And beats it against his leg

The chocolate particles
Substance of life
Cascading earthwards
Leaving their former owner lifeless

Not unlike the day
The eminent puller
Himself
Would be pulled

42 Years

For 42 years we felled the same red oaks, pulled the same
white-faced calves, watered the same corn, laughed at the
same jokes, smelled the same hogs, watched the same sunsets,
cursed the same cloudless July sky, fixed the same busted
bearings, choked on the same August dust, dug the same
October peanuts, attended funerals of the same friends,
climbed the same silos, drove too fast down the same lane,
got stuck in the same places in the same fields, used the same
cramming stick, built the same fence, used the same hammer,
worked in the same hurricane, picked grapes from the same
vine, heard the same thunder…and now you want me to do
it alone?

December

Last year
At this time
Our father was living

We reminisced
About the farm year

He talked of the soil
And the seed
And the land

His arms moved
Though shaking
And he walked
With halting steps

His eyes watered
With memories
Though he fought
It back

He could still
Hear the cattle lowing
The thunderstorm
The Martin

He still
Reveled in life
And the magnificence
Of it all

Today
He lies buried
In a cemetery

In town
His footsteps
No longer
Mark the soil
He worked

His eyes
No longer
Gaze west
At the horizon

He
No longer asks
"What did you get done today?"

Peach Tree

He planted it the spring of '13
The earth emerging from hibernation
As the daffodil made his debut
And the soil smelled clean

Four years hence
Having paid her dues
The twice colored fruit, fully ripened
Releases its fingers
And makes the final descent

But the nurturer
The caretaker
The husbandman
Is not here to savor the crop

Nor was he here to smell the spring rain

He was not here to ride in the white truck and give verdict
on the fields as the corn spiraled through, the peanuts cracked
their ceiling and cotton unfurled its umbrellas

He was not here to stroll amongst the cattle as they raised
their heads with looks of fondness

He was not here to deliver Jack shear bolts at the Copeland
farm

And now, it is July, and he is still not here

Nor will he be here when the combine rolls into the field
and that first ear slides into the throat of the green machine.
We will not see the gleam in his eyes nor the quickening in
his step, that harvest stride, of all the years past

Nor will he be here when the cows get out, the bearing breaks, the tire goes flat, the yoke cracks, the blades need sharpening, the motor runs hot, the auger quits turning and the axle collapses

Nor will he be here to stand in awe as another October sun slips behind his farm, framing fresh dug peanuts as the aroma unfurls

Nor will he be here to dream of the year to come

For he is not here

So eat your peach

And wipe those tears off your cheeks lest someone see them

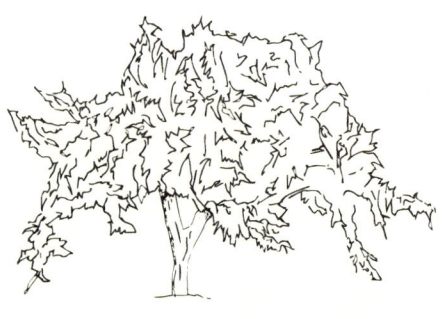

Together

I dream of those days our blood flowed
Together
As we buckled under the August sun
Together
And grabbed another weed
That had the audacity to blemish a peanut field

It was in those days we cleared another acre
Together
And brought a small piece of land into cultivation
Together
As we combed the surface for renegade roots
And wondered the texture of the newfound soil

Back then we brought liquid from the river
Together
And changed well laid plans
Together
As a thirsty crop was king
Much to the chagrin of our wives

That was when we fixed fence on Sunday morn
Together
And pondered
Together
Of what sort venture would next ensnare our yearning
To make the land more beautiful

In that day we pulled a calf
Together
And built a shelter
Together
As the season flew by once again
And we captured another for our memories

And now the silence of solitude and being
Alone
Shapes the substance of thought towards the unfamiliar
Alone
Bequeaths not half a life but another

That desires to hold on to the former
Only to find there is nothing to grasp
But echoes of the past
And a haunting of what was

As the clouds pile high
And the river lopes around the bend
And the Mourning Dove coos
And the willow sways
And the Martin swoops

As if they didn't care

Next Time

Let me die first

Let the pain of loss
Be borne
By the living

Let another
Weep
With inner silence
As memories
Do their razing
And the pile of years
Bury the rememberer

Let that horrid
Emptiness
Indwell another

Let another reminisce
With western sky
And its once shared sun

Let another
See the well worn hoe
The gifted tie
The former garden

Yes, let that one
Succumb to
What once was
And know hopelessness
Of cure
Let me die first

Currents

In this sea of emotion
Random currents
Carry their rudderless
Sailor
To uncharted
Destinations
Where waves
Of despair
Proclaim their
Dominion
With threats of
Inundation

Yet such tides
Are nudged along
By the breath of God
Who sends no
Sojourner
To such place
He has not dwelt

Destiny's Cup

Dumped
Onto the land
Like dice
He and I

Vision clearing
We stagger upright
Gather
It all in

Our lot
Our position
Our place

To spread
Our dreams
And run

Run with the rain
And the wind
And the snow

Run with liberty
And looseness
And laughter

Run for miles
And seasons
And years

Catching
A day
At a time

Filleting it
Savoring it

'Til the dark
Shoves the light
Behind the horizon

And we surrender
Our bodies
To the night

Waiting for
Another chance

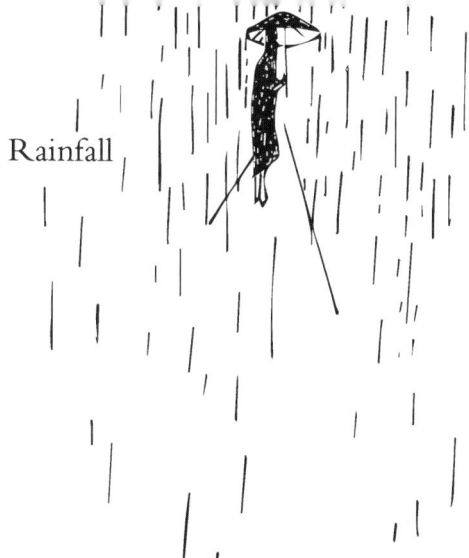

Rainfall

This pond of grief
Filled to its brim
Waits

Takes but a glance
A scent
A distant note

And the dam
That gallant dam
Weakens

Letting its contents spill
Just a bit
Relieving the pressure

As the owner
Rushes to mend
The fissure

Lest the trickle
Become a torrent
And drown its possessor

It lurks again
Nipping at the bank
Waiting for the next rainfall

Cessation of Life

Cessation of life?
Who the hell
Came up with that?

This birth to burial
Passage to dirt
As screaming passions
Become whispers
And that incessant knock at the door
Is muffled
With time

And what of the bonds?
Have they no weight?

Busted asunder
In one fell swoop
Crevasses of nothing
Left that way
For the living remnant
To inhabit and go on

This mockery
Of a thumping heart–
Some eternal play
Casting its actors aside
For a fresher troupe
As the deafening "tick"
And the roaring "tock"
Do their just duty

But then again
Maybe we brought it on ourselves

Late Again

Squeezing the last minutes
Out of the day
As our wives
Watch the cornbread
Grow cold

Rushing in
The back door
Cats scampering
Unlacing boots

Each providing
A buffer for the other
Against the cold chills
Of a woman's wrath

We say grace
The conversation turns
To the day's
Accomplishments
And plans for another

As our perpetual
Tardiness
Dissipates
Between the butterbeans
And the corn

Much to My Dismay

Much to my dismay, it appears the cows are still chewing yesterday's fescue, the wheat sowed down twice its length shows itself, the wind comes predominantly from the southwest, red oaks reach up, the Martins wing their flight, calves chalk their faces, geese play their sky-seat tunes, water is still wet, winter follows fall. How dare it all continue

Tearcatcher

Would there were
A plant
With such a
Name

Could take
This liquid grief
Upon its leaves

And bring forth beauty
Where none was

Next Tuesday

Next Tuesday
A year ago
He left us

Would think
Such time
Would be
Sufficient

To get on
With it

Hell,
A whole crop
Has come
And gone

Four seasons
Passed through the sky
Like tumbleweed

Sold a crop
Of calves

Broke a bearing
In the Milton Field
And fixed it

Sweated out
Two dry spells

Savored
A sip of
Moonshine

Danced
With a trace
Of his loins

But here I am
Weeping
Another damn time

Old Reruns

That haunted,
Screaming past
More real than present
Stabs one with scissors
In the aorta

As debilitating memories
Flood the floor
And coagulate
'Round the coffee table leg

At least there they may die
Or suffocate without oxygen
Or starve without food

But,
Powerless,
I stretch out my palm
And feed them

Enigma

To understand
Is to realize
One can't

Survival

Sometimes the whole sweep
Of his grand history comes
Flooding over me

The years
The 365 times
Crammed into
One memory

Grabbing me
By the throat
And stealing my breath

As I gasp
And shudder
And silently
Scream

And, somehow,
Go on breathing

Chopping Wood

My father taught me every piece
Has a split already started
If one looks close enough

The "whap!" sound
Splinters the air
As another victim
Lies exposed

Lying backside
Upon the ground
Its heart
Rent

By a stronger
Substance

Not unlike
My own

Gulag

Forced into labor
Made to shoulder
That which they
Could never begin to bear

Yet beckoned all the same
Drafted one by one
Ordered into formation
And hoisted upon

Their piteous cries
Ignored
As more are
Shoved into line

For how can the stain of pen
Scaffold the burdens of men?

:: II ::

The Backyard

I sit here
Watching that confounded TV
Shut my mind down with
Other people's thoughts

While trolling
With restive thumb
Searching for the
Utopian channel

As the world consummates
Outside
With intrinsic
Union

The Vireo
Whistles her love song
As the wind
Strums her strings

On the leaves
Of the Pin Oak
And the fescue
Caresses her slim fingers

Between the canopied
Clover
Like two lovers
Gazing at the stars

Content on just being

Foggy Mornings

The world closes in as
The gray soup
Fills in the valleys
And overflows
To the hillsides

Seeping
Through the forests
Like angel hair
Winging its way

Determined
To leave no pocket
Unoccupied
No crevasse
Uninhabited

Even now
I feel it
Tapping
On my window

Morning Rain

Guarded by
This wooden castle
The play unfolds
In freer air

The droplets
Waking us
With their dance
Among the blades

Like a warm blanket
Their rooftop chorus
Seducing our senses

And coaxing us
Back into our soft
Dreams

Where old men
Do not die
Memories do not dim
And I am running
With my sister
Again

The Third Day

Not
What
You
Think

For no one's
Rising from
The Dead

But rather snowed in
The tranquil cover
Now violated
By footprints

The whiteness
Losing its
Novelty

As the
Familiar walls
Press
Inward

And
Standard
Schedules
Scream for
Sovereignty
Once again

Thrown into
A drift
We are

As the birds
And clouds
Laugh at our
frailties

Cows

Their cliquish
Meeting
Subtly
Called

Would love
To be
In
Inner Circle

Perhaps
Rumblings
Of jealousy

As mothers do
What mothers do
With their genius offspring

The captain of the harem
Cuddles his chew
Close by

A distance in his eyes
He wallows in
The previous night's
Shenanigans

:: III ::

Awakened

It's 2 AM.
I lie here
Listening to the cadenced
Respire of my bride

The air
Purses the lips,
Makes its
Splendid journey
And returns

I wonder
What visions
Lie behind
The shuttered
Lids

She speaks!
The tongue
Unhinged from reticence
Erupts in freedom

I listen
With stiffened body
To her uncensored
Heart

"Rex" was first utterance
My weak heart missed a beat
But then my world imploded
With the words, "I smell your feet"

Dissenter

Traveling across the plains
It rises up
From the nothingness

A renegade
Rebelling against
The landscape

It sits there
In defiance
Unashamed
Unabashed

Yet beautiful
Exclusive
As it pierces
The atmosphere
Setting
Its own boundaries

Such breaks
In the terrain
Invites its own mystique

Shall I ever
Be enthralled
With that mole
Upon her cheek?

Traveling

I have kissed the wind
According to my calculations
It is coming your way
And should arrive at 9:13 pm

With that kiss
Is part of my heart
And part of my soul
So brace yourself!
It is weighty and

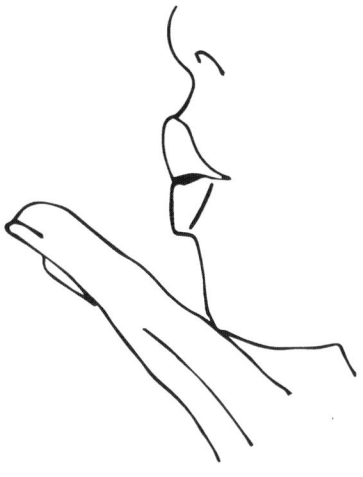

I do not want you to get hurt
For it arrives
With speed
And can be cushioned

Only
By lips such as yours
Which were made for mine
If my math is correct

Trickery

I called her
And she did not answer
Again

What a fool
I am
And have been

To again
Be defeated
By my own heart

That tricks me
Time and again
Thinking

Another human being
Could possibly
Consider me
A viable option

Tell Me

Tell me
I sometimes
Slip into
Your dreams
And run with you
And we are both alive
Very much alive
There's all the world
In that dream
And then there's us
Only us
As our senses
Intertwine
Like basket weaving
And our voices
Frolic with words
Like spring calves
And then you awake
Panting
Straining
To get back in
That dream

Tell me

Tarriance

He picked his way
Haltingly
As the Trail
Narrowed

And obscured
The sojourner's sight
With overgrowth
That strangled
his view

What began
As a downhill jaunt
Over which
He had drifted along

Had mutated
To an incline
Of increasing
Difficulty

Glancing back
The trail
Had already
Grown over
Preventing any
Retracing of steps

Surely
Around the bend
A more tolerable terrain
Would emerge

He lay down
To rest

Unhinged

Divorced from
Farm life
The rhthym
Broken

Life takes on
A different hue
As we skate
Hotel to hotel

Weaving our
Web of memories

Landscape and accents
Changing
As the roar of the road
Unlaces the corset
From home

"Charolais cattle"
She points out

She has brought
A bit of home
With us

I revel my bride
Has adopted
Such lingo

Perhaps

One time, long ago
   I brushed your skin...
      Perhaps it was a nothing
         On your part
            But my skin interpreted it
            Otherwise
               And imagined
                  Deliberateness
                  From you
                     Though I'm sure
                     You didn't
                        Give a damn
                        Because when
                           You walked away
                           You never
                           Looked back

Beauty

They run from
Just outside the neck
On the backside
Down to the 11th rib

The left goes up
Like a chart of a company
That had a very good third quarter
On the right
A quarter of losses

Fleshly mountain ranges
Formed through
Cataclysmic events
That altered the
Landscape

While their owner
Lay asleep
Letting the surgeon
Do his deft work

Fifteen years hence
Though witnessed only
At the seaside
And between bathroom and closet

They parade her beauty
All the more
Branded, if you would
My bride of valor

:: IV ::

Gravity

Were it not for gravity, slides would not work
Nor would peeing off the back porch
Though I thought I was alone
Freely exercising my mannish freedom

Watching the singular waterfall
Disrupt the mulch
With a great flood
And little canoes

Swept along the white water
Banging the sides
Trying to stay afloat
John Wesley Powellish

My bride, peering through the bedroom glass
At my backside
Snickering
Though I think she was envious

Life Across the Bridge

From whence do they come?

The horizon spits them out
As its belly heaves
A rhythmic churn

These crashing, rolling
Tubes of liquid
Placating cochlea
With their symphonic tune

The ankles, then the thighs
Succumb to invitation
Drenching their recipient
With earth's sweat

As each makes its ordered retreat
And takes mortal's unending cares
Down into the depths
Where they are drowned-
Drowned, I tell you!

The former owners, unencumbered,
Raise the victor's glass!
The weightlessness intoxicates,
"Let's kick them in the ass!"

Freedom has its luxuries
What views atop the ridge!
But somber resurrection strikes
Returning 'cross the bridge

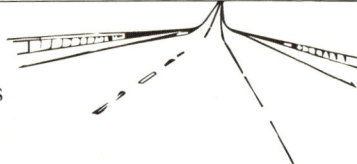

Vacation List

Does this Admiral not rule the seas?
Sending his lieutenants
Scurrying about
With such particular orders?

Don't forget the coffee
Don't forget the keys
Don't forget the baking soda
'Case you're stung by bees

Don't forget the charcoal
Don't forget the fan
Don't forget the glue and tape
'Case you're Piltdown Man

Don't forget the games
Don't forget the meds
Don't forget the gluten free
'Case it's in your bread

Don't forget the matches
Don't forget your hon'
Don't forget to write back home
To prove you're having fun

Now it sits motionless
In the back of the top
Drawer
Of a wooden desk
Court–martialed

The Tip Jar

Mr. Mason would be glad
Knowing his sealable reservoir of preservation
Was in fact
Catapulting Ginny
From the 80% that own 5%
To the 5% that own 80%

The rectangular mouth
Beseeching a swig
Of Laissez-faire

Its transparent belly
Gloating
As George
Peers from the chamber
Leaning against Abraham sitting on Thomas

While Ginny
Lets her eyes
And her innocence
Do all the work

Dominoes

One lays out words like dominoes
Trying to find the next perfect brick

As chests fall against backs
The former tackling the latter

Not really knowing where they are going
(For it is difficult to see over another's shoulder)
But each endeavoring to do their part
Whatever the position

So the whole team
Exhausted
Laid out and spent
Wins

For if one doesn't
It ends

Crestfallen

'Tis January
Two thousand
Eighteen years
Since the birth

But not mine
Only 62 years
Since a birth

That
Initiated no calendars
Wars
Or holidays

But only
The wail
Of a crying
Infant

Upon hearing
The doctor
Declare

"We need
To put
This one
Back"

His parents
Longing
For a daughter

Turning Point

A formal climate
It was
The stately ladies filing into
The living room

As the Woman's Club
Sounded the gavel
And commenced
To addressing
Their noble business

While a lad of seven
Slipped into
Adjacent room
And commenced
To addressing
His noble business

The amber stream
Gushing into the reservoir
From upward height
Making water symphony
A full fourteen seconds

Which wafted through
The uninsulated wall
And sliced through
The discussion
On the February fundraiser

Much
To
The
Mother's
Horror

After which
She addressed
Her offspring's
Unconscionable behavior

Much
To
The
Son's
Horror

Changed the course of history
This lesson so applied
Today at 62
He always hits the side

Coasting

Easier to read another
Watch another
Set the furrow
Hoist the hay

Observe
Another's pain
Under roof
Bereft of rain

Regard
The choir spew
Nestled
In the pew

Far less difficult
To run the race
Set the pace
Participate
Vicariously

Exiled

Anathema to
This never
Ceasing
Exaggeration

Every tale
Embellished
Every superlative
Deified

Were I to pen
A thousand books
In a thousand tongues

Let my
Left hand
Be stricken
With the venom
Of paralysis

And my right
Severed
At the
Wrist

If I stoop
To castrate
Language
In such manner

Sanctification

I can hear her
Talking on the phone
In the next room
To my sister

Who always gets
Right to the point
But they are
Good points

Like stars
But there are
A lot of stars

And the leap
From one to another
Is unsettling
Like walking
On air
Not sure
Where one
Might land

Flying
Floundering
Flouncing about

Searching
For someplace–
Anyplace!–
To land forever

But even now
Glancing down

I sense the quiver
Of the ground

Guests

The New Year forces
It's way in
Kicking its
Older brother
Aside

He sweeps
The past
Off the back porch
Into a clutter
Of disappointments

The good intentions
Mangled
Upon the
Self control

And sets up shop
Commissioning his staff

Hope
Takes the room upstairs
Surprise
The in-law suite
While optimism
Strums a tune
In the corner
That settles
Like dust

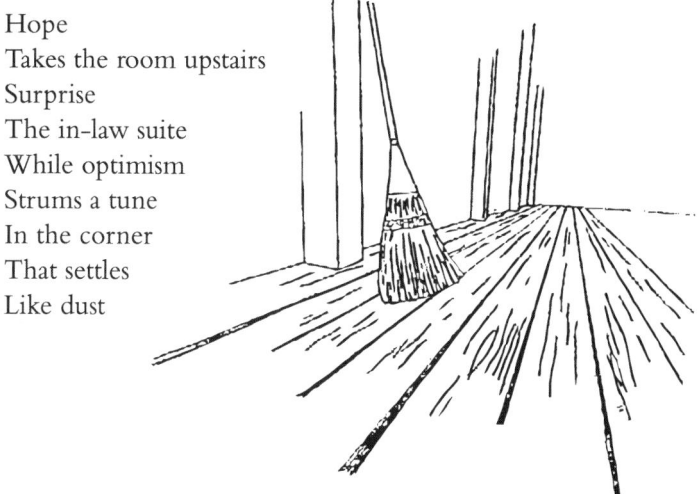

Sibling Rivalry

The index
The teacher's instrument
The disciplinarian's rod
Often going solo

While the middle
The taller brother
Glories in its dominance
Especially when standing alone

Though its companion
The ring
Carries the banner
Of commitment

And the runt of the litter
At the end of the bench
Follows the family
Like an obedient son

Which leaves the opposing
Appendage
Captain of the grasp
Heckling his siblings
While they envy his design
See how he even gets another line?

Fissure

An old family narrative, regurgitated, once again

"Did we do that?" she asks with
perplexed eyes, though not the least perturbed

She does not remember

Turning, she discharges her generous duty with shaking
hands,
fumbling with the Reynolds Wrap

"I made some fudge this morning. Take some to your
meeting"

I, the gift bearer, comply

Another brick cascades down as the foundation shivers,
but the wall holds, with nine decades of mortar

For how long?

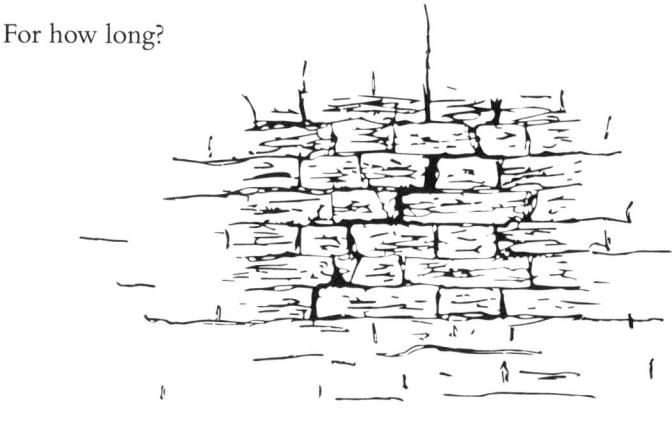

The Return

Hurling across
The earth's surface
On ribbons of asphalt
At miles per minute

Parting the trees
Nicely seated
in our cocoon
Of steel

We touch
The stars
In their orbit

Abilene…Jackson…Johnson City…

Our own meteor
Circling down
Through the universe
Returning to
Its mother lode

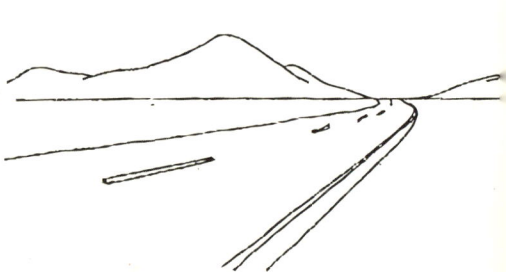

Skimming above
The surface
Of troubles
For a time

We propel
Down
Down
Down

To the source of it all

And land,
At last
In the rich soil
Of Sunset View

Ode to Texas After 5 Days and 4 Nights in a Hotel

Having found the perfect coordinates
For the long chrome handle that
Turns to the right
Blending the opposite waters
Just such

Having deduced
The second pillow
Next to the headboard
Best suited for night

And Frosted Flakes
Pulled from the bottom
With 2% and cardboard bowl

Having mastered
The expulsion
Of the last
Of the conditioner

And connecting with Monica
Eight months in
At the front desk

And Linda
Two years strong
Bringing in
A second batch of links

The local paper
Top left shelf
With comics
The national
To the right

We pack up
And head to another town

Silence

Seems
To make
Us
A bit
Uncomfortable

For nothing
Is getting done

No words
Being passed around
No nails being driven
No clanking of plates being washed
No combustible engines
Combusting

No scintillating debate
No catapults of hate
No mischief in the air
No squeaking of the chair

No cities being built
No squares on the quilt
No symphonic tones
No lovemaking moans

No shrieks of adulation
No groans of aggravation
No gulping down the pill
No sizzling on the grill

No ticking of the clock
No mesmerizing Bach
No humming of the road

No beeping bar code

Only silence
Is getting done

Eyes

There is much
We do not see

The spiders
Flying through the air
The old men
Crying in despair
Cow giving birth in pain
Synapses connecting the brain

The chirp in the forest
The lonely guitarist
The seahorses' eyes
The discarded French fries

The missing heartbeat
The mother's defeat
The Canada Goose call
The spilt alcohol

The doctor's diagnosis
Our own halitosis
The shattered heart
Last of Snellen chart

Longing
Grief
Yearning
Desperation

God, give us eyes…

Run With Me

So where are the poems?
That frolic with words
That noticing
The never noticed?

Have the "finer"
Things in life
Those imposters of reality
Charmed your restless hearts?

So you both
Consume your seconds
With that dreadful
Word called maintenance?

Come
Play with me!
As we did
In the bin
When ten

Let the wings of words
Give you flight!
There are worlds
Yet to be visited!

Come Ruffin
Come Trena
Run with me
Once again!

Bleeding

My life bleeds
Through my pen

"Your writing is very personal"
They said.
Perhaps too
But how else
Can I leave you
A part of me?

Lest I take it all
To the grave
And give away nothing
But an old pair of jeans

Who would want those?

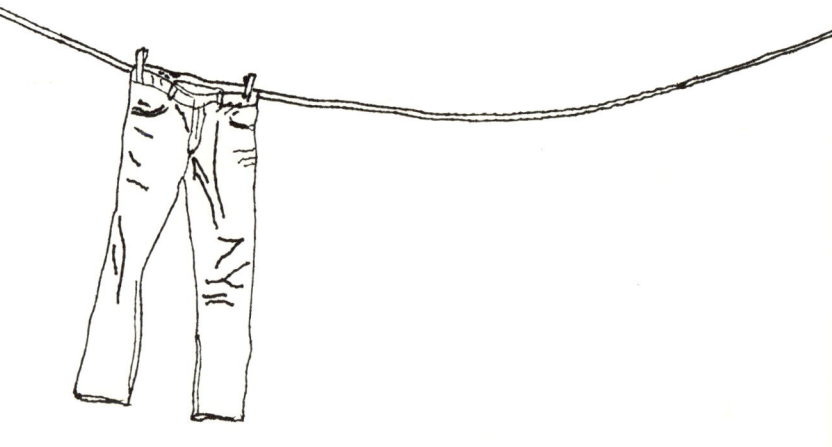

Acknowledgment

A special thanks to my son, though imbedded across the sea in that grand island, worked countless hours editing, suggesting, exploring alternatives, re-editing and sending me many proofs for this work. No doubt, he too loved my father, his grandfather. Thank you, Judson.